SARAH TUCK
CREATIVE WRITING JOURNEY

SARAH TUCK

Front Cover – pictured along with myself are from left to right:

Top Right to Left: Alice Bailey, Myself and Nancy Combow

Second Row: Stephon Bowmen Jr., Jane Lewis, and Bennett Gatewood

Lisa Deavers and Cynthia Ford

Inita Rippy and Kristie Stratton

Copyright © 2020 by Sarah Tuck

This is a work of true story. Names, characters places and incidents either are the product of the author's real-life story or are true events. These names of a few actual persons, living or dead were changed to protect the innocent and the events, or locale is entirely true.

All rights reserved. No part of this book may be reproduced or used in any manner without written permission of the copyright owner except for the use of quotations in a book review.

Sarah Tuck Book for adults/18-years and older Readers/Authorship:

Book Manufactured in United States of America

First Edition

Library of Congress in Publication Data

ISBN: 9780578686844 (paperback)

ISBN: 9780578687568 (e-book)

Table of Contents

Chapter 1: Sarah Tuck Creative Writing Journey 1

Chapter 2: I Traveled To Louisville, Kentucky For The Next Play .. 17

Chapter 3: I Traveled To Gallatin, Tennessee To Recruit 25

Chapter 4: Started Writing My First Book 44

Chapter 5: Traveled To Bowling Green, Kentucky For The Next Play 56

Chapter 6: Honored For The Strathmore's Who's Who Book 65

Chapter 7: Attending My First Book Signing 78

Chapter 8: Starting The New Year Off On Television January 1, 2020 92

Chapter 9: First Annual Valentines Author Event 99

Afterword 117

About The Author 118

1

SARAH TUCK CREATIVE WRITING JOURNEY

The story you are about to read is a true story of Sarah Tuck, "Creative Writing Journey." We have changed a few of the names to protect the innocent.

Foremost, she would like to give praise to God for all the "Blessings" that they have been given to her by her beautiful parents; "Mr. Willie Douglas Edison and Lillian Lee West-Edison."

She has been through major storms in her life, for the losing, of two husbands of which you will read about later on in her story.

Through all this, she has raised her loving and devoted daughter Ms. Lauren Tuck, whom she thanks God for each day.

Come take this trip with her back down memory lane to see how far she has come in being obedient to God's words to her.

Her journey started several years before she stepped out on faith to write her creative work. She was already writing and sharing her work with some of her friends.

When one day two of her girlfriends told her she needed to become a writer. Especially on this one particular day, Ms. Jo-Ann Smith mentioned to her saying, "You need to write a book."

That's how well they loved hearing her read some things she had wrote.

She replied, "People don't want to read what I write."

Jo-Ann said, "But, I'm telling you could write a book, girl."

Then later on in her life, things change. The day came when she was faced with some difficulties in her life where she started praying, asking God for over seven-years. What is her purpose for being here?

I know you are wondering why was she asking, "God this question?"

Follow her in this story while she explains to you why she asked God this question.

Let's go back to the place and time where all this took place in a small community of Franklin, Kentucky where I was born and raised.

This is the reason I asked God this question in May 2007.

Way before I asked this question…I had lost two husbands in death.

Yes, this was troubling me so much I wanted to understand why.

This is when I went constantly into praying for seven years asking, God please show me my purpose for being here while my two husbands had gone.

I was feeling God left me here for a special purpose since this had happened to me twice. But I couldn't rest until I had some kind of confirmation from God on what was going on.

The first time this happened to me I lost my husband Andre Tuck to leukemia on July 28, 1993. This devastated me to the point I didn't know what to do. God left me here with a four-year-old daughter to take care of by myself at thirty-three years old, and he was thirty-six years old.

I knew this would not be easy, trying to explain to a four-year-old that her daddy would never come back home again.

Each day for weeks my daughter sat on the couch looking at the living room door, watching and waiting for her daddy to come through that door.

I tried in so many ways to comfort her the best way that I knew how.

I gave her toys to play with, sang to her, and even gave her hugs, and, kisses only to see that this wasn't enough. It broke my heart to see her like this.

I didn't give up on her, I kept on praying, trying to work with her as much as I could.

Till one day she just started playing with her toys, laughing being herself once again. This is when I had a sigh of relief.

Now it was time for me to grieve because I realized he wasn't ever coming back through those doors ever again.

I knew that I had to keep it together to take care of our daughter and myself.

Each day, I got up to take a step in learning how to live without the man…that I had slept beside me and woke up with me…for almost ten years, ever since we married.

It would take some getting used to but, through praying, crying and the will power of God, I had to do this.

I wasn't only doing this for me but for the sake of me being a mother to our daughter, and for my late husband Andre.

Andre was so proud of the accomplishments that I made throughout our marriage. I remember the day he said, "I will take care of the bills for six months and then I want you to take care of the bills for the next six months."

This way, if something ever happens to one of us, we will be able to manage without the other one not being here.

I knew what he meant by that statement so I didn't disagree, I just listen to what he had to say.

So, from that day forward, we both took turns bringing our share to the table and handing it over to the other one to make sure things work.

We were young in love and we both wanted something in life.

I realize now by doing this helped me prepare for the day I was faced with his death.

You never know when God is preparing a foundation for you to build with someone, this is why we all need to listen and pay attention to what's going on in our lives.

Always remember what works for one couple may not work for another without prayer.

Then is when you will understand why these things happen the way they do in our lives.

As the years went by, I had to cope and learn how to manage my life without my husband not being there. But I could never forget him because every day that I looked at our daughter, I could see a part of him.

When a year had passed, my family and friends were worried about me and felt like I might need to go out on a date sometimes.

So, two friends and family members set me up on a blind date a few times.

I tried it a few times, but it wasn't the same.

Not until I was introduced to this gentleman by one of my cousins who I thought could maybe be the one for me.

When only I found out after several years of dating him…he was not the one for me.

I only have this to say, "Never co-sign for anyone."

Then thirteen years later from losing Andre I was introduced to another gentleman named Robert Waggoner.

We went out to lunch one day and talked for hours.

From that day forward we kept in contact until the day he asked me to marry him. I accepted his proposal got married and we became as one.

Then I was no longer alone after that.

We got married on April 29, 2005, here in my hometown Franklin, Kentucky.

We were happy enjoying life for almost a year then until one day I received a call while I was waiting for him to come and pick me up for Bible study on a Wednesday afternoon on April 11, 2006.

When the phone rang, the call was from one of my step-daughters calling me crying, when I asked, "What was wrong?" She then told me that her dad was dead he had died in a truck accident.

I was once again devastated for the second time in losing another one of my husbands.

As I laid down the phone, I called my mother and told her I was standing there in shock.

All I could do, was think of why did this happen to me for the second time? Then I said, "What have I done to have this happen to me twice?"

Then I took my seat, and while I was sitting there trying to get a grip on what had just happened, I heard mama at the door and asked her to come in.

I was still sitting there in shock, wondering, "How could this have happened to me."

Then one of my sisters came to the door and my mother went over to the door to let her in. She had called her before coming over to let her know what had happened.

Then I said, "I need to go to Munfordville, Kentucky to check on my step-children to comfort them."

If you notice, I wasn't thinking of myself as I had done before. It was my duty to make sure that the children were all alright first."

I then got into my car and traveled there to check on them late that evening. I then came back to my home to find family, friends, and church members there to comfort me.

Once again, I faced having to let go of my loved one right just before we could celebrate our first anniversary.

With prayer, faith and the will power of God, I could get through this tragedy once again.

I was eager to find out why.

Through faith and praying for seven years, I finally found out what my purpose was to still be here in the land of the living.

This is when I felt like I was chosen to use my creative writing to touch and help others in this walk of life.

I'm still writing every chance I get to create what God has given me to write to touch other people's lives along the way of my amazing journey.

Come and go with me and let's see the steps that I have taken by being obedient to God, ordering me to step out on faith since May 17, 2014.

Before God had come to me on that day, I had started writing a book on my life. I had written about eight pages when I heard God's voice speaking to me saying, "It's your time step out."

Then I looked around and said, "Right now…but, I'm writing my book on my life."

But I remembered what my pastor had told our congregation one Sunday. When God speaks to you to tell you to do something don't ask questions, just step out on faith and do it.

Shortly afterward, I called another one of my friends to explain to her about the experience that I had just had with God.

I then mention to her that I wanted to start writing plays.

She told me to talk to this other lady that has been writing plays and she was a writer too.

I looked up her number to call her then I asked her could I come over to meet with her on what God had given me to do. Her reply was sure you can come on this day and I will talk to you then.

You could tell in her voice that she was getting excited about what I was telling her over the phone.

On the day that I arrived, she was patiently waiting for me to come over. I ranged the doorbell, then she let me in and we sat down and started talking. I talked with her, and showed her the ten different plays that I wanted to write.

As she was looking them over and listening to me speak about the experience that I had just had with God.

She made a statement to me and she thought she was the only one running around here with things like this going on in her head. Sometimes she said, "I feel like people are looking at me like I'm weird."

That's when I said, "Now you are not by yourself, this is happening to me now."

We laughed and continued talking about writing our first play together.

Our conversation went on for a while; then I was told to go home write my half while she would write half, then we were to meet back up together in a week.

And this is just what we did. We did this for several weeks until we finally had written a play together.

This is when I considered her to be my mentor.

She told me that my next step was to recruit some actors for the play.

This is what I did when we held our first audition on June 22, 2014.

We didn't have that many to show up, but; we were happy with the ones that came.

Since there wasn't enough to attend on that day, we had to hold another audition on July 20, 2014.

The strangest thing happened though, to my mentor, she wasn't able to attend.

So, I just went right on with the audition and continued to move fast forward in getting the rehearsal for the play schedule in doing everything else that I needed to do.

When one day I met this young lady called Mis'Shan Dunn while she was at my house visiting my daughter.

I told her about the play. Then I asked her if she would be interested in being in the play and her two children. She agreed, and they came to our next rehearsal.

I was glad to have her, Jayden Johnson, and Ebony Cargile joining the production.

Then suddenly, after several months had passed, I then scheduled the play for November 2014. Meanwhile, I had heard that some people were talking about bringing, "Black Art plays" to Franklin, Kentucky.

So, this is when I went to talk with someone about the plans I had on having a play in Franklin.

The person I had gone to see did not want to use my play, but she said, "If you could get an organization to back you, then maybe you can accomplish putting this play on."

She said, "Make sure you reach out to some local businesses to support you with some donations, this will help you with putting on your play."

Immediately, I left their office and contacted Ms. Wanda Tuck with the "Franklin Simpson Human Rights Commission." Ms. Wanda said, "Yes, we would be more than glad to support this play."

I was pleased with Ms. Wanda Tuck and the Franklin Simpson Human Rights Commission wanting to help me with my play. Ms. Wanda Tuck even added me to the Franklin Simpson Human Rights Commission Newsletter on the front page.

This gave me such great pleasure to see me featured on this organization's Newsletter.

Since this helped me to make connections with people across the State of Kentucky.

This has given me the opportunity to open doors that I didn't think that I could open.

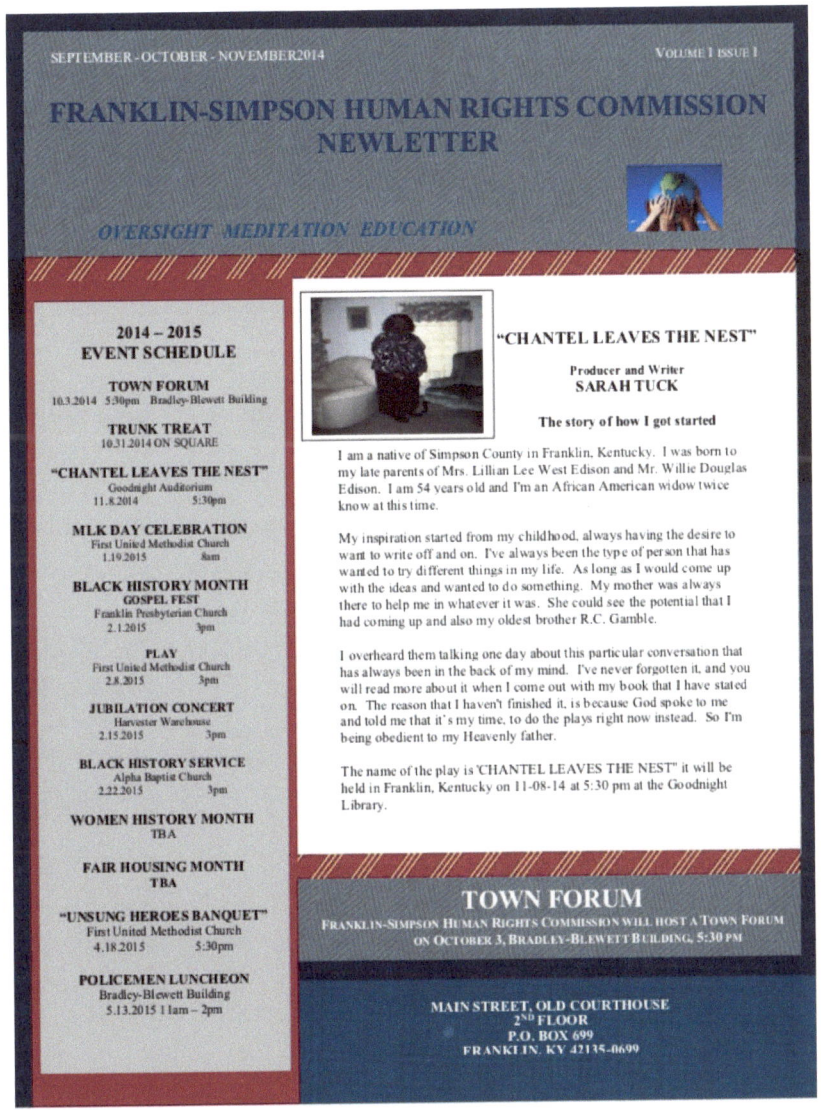

Then I left there to use the advice on contacting some local businesses to ask them for help in sponsoring my play.

Let me remind you these were some places I had done business with before, or my parents or husband had done business with them. But when I asked them, I was turned away with a lot of them letting me down.

I only had 2 businesses to give me a donation to help me with my play here in my hometown.

There were a few personal donations that were given to me from here and the rest was from out-of-town businesses.

Now you don't think I stopped there, do you?

Well, no I didn't I contacted WBKO television station to see if I could go on there to let the people know about my play.

I was accepted and gave my first television interview on November 3, 2014.

I remembered when I was young, I had made the statement one day that I was going to be on television. Now finally the dream had come true.

Not only did I make the television show later in November 2014, I was talking on the radio station at 100.7.

Then it happened I was finally having my play on stage at the Goodnight Library.

The young lady who appears on this flyer…is Nancy Uhls, who played as the character Chantel.

She has been a resident of Franklin, Kentucky for 28 years.

Nancy is married to Benny Ray Uhls and is the mother of four children and six grandchildren.

She works as a Nuclear Medicine & Radiation Safety Officer and she is the owner of A Healing Touch Massage Therapy.

I was glad to see all the people who came out to support us.

On this day I saw so many people it touched my heart, my mentor, and my actors as well.

Then it happened; the show started, and before it was over I joined them later on stage to sing a song.

When the play was over the audience stood up and gave us a standing ovation. This is when I realized that this was my purpose that God had planned for me.

I then came down off the stage and walked over to some of my friends that were there, to thank them for being there on this special night to support us. Then I asked how they like the show.

When they started complimenting us on the performance, this is when my eyes lit up and a great big smile came across my face when I heard how much they loved the show.

They even made statements of how they thought they were at a Broadway show. This made me feel even more proud of what my mentor and I had done.

The cast was excited too, especially about the reception that the "Franklin Simpson Human Rights Commission" were giving us after the play.

The reception was being held at another building this is why they were changing and getting ready to leave to go over there for the party.

So, I told everyone to go ahead while I made sure the building was cleaned up and to make sure the gentleman retrieved all his sound equipment.

When all of this was done, the building was locked up. I then proceeded to go over to the place where the reception was being held.

I arrived at the place where the party was going on; then got out of the car with my cousin, and went in and spoke to everyone, then we took our seat.

I was worn out from all the preparations that I had done in getting this play off the ground.

While I was sitting there, I noticed some of the people had already left, I didn't even get a chance to say anything to them.

But, my mentor did, she had come over and started talking to me about some of the things they had told her about how much they liked the play.

Even some of the ones that were still there gave me compliments on how good the play was.

My mentor then leaned over and whispered to me, "I'm clipping your wings as of tonight."

I then spoke up and said, "Oh no, you can't do that. I don't think that I'm ready to be by myself."

My mentor replied, "If I see that you are falling from the nest…I will pick you up, and put you back in the nest. But, you are going to do just fine."

I was surprised in what I had heard while I was sitting there in disbelief that she would do this to me.

But this is when I realized that God had to be leading her to tell me that it was time for me to fly away you got this now.

By realizing this miracle that God had showed me on this day I could see why my mentor wasn't able to be there with me during this whole time.

I later felt like I was being tested for my strength and ability of what all I could do. As the scripture says in "Philippians 4:13, "I can do all things through him who strengthens me."

Many things happen for a reason in a season that we don't have control over, nor do we understand.

This is why my mentor was ill, and couldn't come to the rehearsals to help me finished the recruiting for the play.

She had done just what God had ordered her to do now it was time for her to step aside and let me go my way because I was ready.

We don't always understand what's going on, but God shows us in his own way of telling us you are not alone and I got you.

I prayed about it and, thought about it, then I walked away with confidence on my new journey of writing and putting together new plays.

As time passed on; I had begun to realize that I had now become a writer, producer, actor, and director of my plays.

This was the greatest feeling that I could ever want to have in this whole wide world.

It's amazing how God will show you your purpose in life, if you just pray and ask him and stay still and be humble long enough for him to reveal it to you.

There were times though that I must admit that I wanted to give up but God wouldn't let me and now I'm glad that I didn't.

2

I TRAVELED TO LOUISVILLE, KENTUCKY FOR THE NEXT PLAY

While I was thinking about what my next step would be, I travel to Louisville, Kentucky to recruit another set of the cast for the next play. The name of this play was "My Son Is Coming Home for Christmas."

I had thought about the idea of this Christmas play after I was approached by someone who mentioned to me they wanted to see a Christmas play.

This is when I gave it a great deal of thought. Then I wrote a Christmas play.

Before I had gone to Louisville to hold the auditions, I travel to

Chattanooga, Tennessee to see if I could get a group established there in May 2015.

But it appeared the people there weren't as interested, or maybe because I wasn't able to reach many people.

I could only recruit two ladies that stayed in touch with me so we could collaborate on another play soon.

The guy I recruit didn't stay in contact with me, so there wasn't enough cast to hold the play there.

I finally accepted the disappointment then moved onto Louisville, Kentucky where I could recruit enough people to put the play on there.

Once again, as I had done before, I posted ads for auditions to recruit cast members for the play.

Then I went looking for a place to hold the audition, then I started having the auditions there in Louisville, Kentucky at the library other times it was in a meeting room of a restaurant.

Some people came, some left, some, even stayed. I was seeing the same pattern again from a few of these members, just as I had before of not wanting to come to rehearsals and quitting after a few rehearsals.

But I had more of them that were faithful in coming to almost every rehearsal.

It was hard to get some people to see where God was leading me with these plays, I was trying so hard to deliver, to touch other people's lives.

I didn't let this get me all the way down, though I just kept right on pushing forward to make this gift work.

I had to remember that God gave the vision to me, not the people, as I was so politely told by a few of my cast members.

So, I carried this out with or without them, because if I didn't, then I would have defeated the purpose of me praying for seven years and asking God to show me my purpose....

This gave me even more confidence in knowing that I was fulfilling the purpose with the gift God had given me.

I only had a few faithful members though, that was seeing what was going on with me.

I had one young lady to come to all most every one of the rehearsal, but a few times she had to leave early.

There were a few that would travel with me to Louisville, Kentucky for the rehearsals until one of them injured their leg.

This is when I had to ask one of my former members, Minister Darren Bush, to help me out in taking the leading role.

In which he was more than glad to do so.

Minister Darren Bush is no stranger to the stage, as he has performed in various churches often acting singing and dancing.

He and his cousin Felicia Bland are the founders of Gifts of Praise, which is a Faith-Based youth arts program in Bowling Green, Kentucky.

For this play, I recruited some men that had been in the service and wanted to work with me in this play. I could see that they knew what to do after I had worked with them. They were enjoying it too.

I remember one of them saying, "I always wanted to act in Performing Arts, so I'm willing to try it."

When the show was over, he approached me and said, "Thank you for the opportunity of being in your play, I enjoyed it and was glad that I did it."

This touched my heart like you wouldn't believe. I could feel the sense of making someone's dreams come true.

Again, this is when I could see my gift from God had made somebody else happy once again.

Shortly before the show, the time came that I was looking for a sound engineer. One of my members suggested someone that I agreed to talk to and see what we could work out.

When I meant with him, I didn't realize that he would be as expensive as he was.

He knew that it was getting close to time to have the show and I was running out of options.

I even explained to him we didn't have a treasurer, just as I had everyone else.

So, I used him anyway, because they had recommended him so highly.

Then we had a rehearsal, and he only came to one practice, and he didn't even stay for the whole practice to see what all he needs I would be instructed to do.

By him leaving early, I knew then things would not go as planned.

My play took place on November 6, 2015, in Louisville, Kentucky. I then proceeded, as usual, preparing the play…then on that very day of the play.

It happened I was very disappointed in the performance that the sound engineer had given me. The music didn't start on time; he played some records before time or not quick enough.

I looked around and said, to myself, "I must be in the twilight zone. I couldn't believe this was happening at this very moment."

His gentleman friend looked at me and could see what I was talking about. He had come with him to assist him.

I wanted to run somewhere and hide, but there was nowhere for me to go.

People don't realize when something goes wrong with the high hope of something that you have worked so hard to expect a good show. It hurts, and all you can do is swallow it and pray that the next time it will be better.

It astonished me in how the crowd liked the performance of the play and still gave us compliments despite all the mistakes we made. Some had mentioned they were looking forward to attending Part II.

Then there were a few that gave fairly nice comments and this is when I felt like I had felled with these people.

Therefore, from then on, I felt like it is very important for each cast member and sound engineer to come to rehearsals, listen for your cues, learn your lines, and do what I asked of you to make sure everything runs smoothly.

Remember, you can't teach someone that isn't present.

I later on, took the play to my hometown in Franklin, Kentucky.

The cast came and put on a great show to the ones that was there; I was a little surprised though on how slim the crowd was.

I later heard there were some other events taking place that day.

Although we were missing a person for the play, I knew I could pull my daughter in to fill in as one of the soldiers.

She is a shy person and had no intention of acting that day.

But she knew that her mama needed her help, so she stepped in and helped us out. That's what family does for each other when the chips are down.

Within the next day or two, I had two of the cast members call me demanding their pay and said some ugly things to me.

As I tried to explain to them how we only had fifteen people in the audience that night, and, the time I paid for the building we had nothing left.

I had even explained to them we didn't have a treasurer, yet therefore I was giving everyone tickets to sell to make sure we could make this play work.

Some came back with their tickets and said, "I couldn't sell them."

I knew then we would not have enough money for everything but, we went on with the play, anyway.

People seem to forget you have to work as a team to make things work. One or two people can't carry all the weight.

When I heard how these two cast members were acting, I was very disappointed in them. I had such high hope of adding them to my books as time passed on and more shows till this took place.

This is when I felt like they were only there for the money, not for the blessing that was yet to come.

If they had held out, they could have been on the front cover of one of my books to share with their family and friends.

One lady even had the nerves to say I took all the credit. I thought this was strange when I had put all the names and pictures on my business page and on the flyers, we had to pass out.

Giving all my members credit for what they were doing, hoping that some producer in the audience could see their performance and ask them to be in their play, movie, commercial, etc.

Sometimes we let the anger come over us and lose the eyesight visible for us to see.

All the other cast members understood and didn't ask me for anything because they could see that we didn't have a big turn-out and money was not the object for them.

They were just glad to be a part of the play and to perform on stage.

Plus, this would have been something that they could have shared in February for Black History month with their church and everyone else.

Again, it's hard to make people see the vision that God has given you.

But since then, one of those cast members has been posting likes on my page and sending me birthday wishes.

I truly feel like this person has realized that they made a mistake in how they reacted to me.

I since then made sure that everyone had even a better understanding of how my company runs.

If you come just to make money, this is not the place for you. I'm in the business for blessing people where God leads me. When you see my plays and read my books…you will better understand where I'm coming from.

I feel like in time God will supply us with the money he wants us to have.

Some people who have not been in the industry, may not understand the business side of profits vs. expenditures, not to exclude labor and professional time spent on such large projects. Such as, writing scripts…that takes money. Something so simple as paper, can be a great expense. Then you have other writing materials, technology, props, production assistance, music composers, etc. So, money may not be an object to some people, but for my dream…it takes every dollar to invest in such a project.

Until then we need to stay humble in using the gifts he has given us to share with others.

This is the gift God gave me to share with the world, my creative work to help make a difference in their life.

I know this is my purpose and I want to continue to do God's will in writing whatever he puts upon my heart to write.

So with this being said, "You may come to join us if you feel the same way and see if God is leading you down the same path."

3

I TRAVELED TO GALLATIN, TENNESSEE TO RECRUIT

Once again it was time to recruit some new cast members for another play, I had written. This time I traveled to Gallatin, Tennessee where my cousin named Mary Mitchell said, "I will help you this time around."

We went downtown to the Theater to check on booking a venue for the play.

Once again things were coming together like before.

There I was planning to recruit my third set of cast members for this play.

Then we went to Mary's house to show her the script of Grandma Mattie Gets Her a Man.

I asked her, "If she would like to take one character."

She replied, "Yes, I'm excited to be joining you in this great opportunity to be in your play, I will do something different now."

We laughed and talked about the plans I had made for the cast members who would join us in this production.

Mary even spoke up for her daughter Monique for me to add her to the list because she could take one character too.

We discussed some ways of recruiting cast members to come out for the audition.

I even contacted a lady there who writes plays, named Betty Ann Britton.

I found out that Betty Ann Britton began her acting career in 1990 and she is SAG (Screen Actor Guild) eligible.

She has been cast in various film and television roles in Nashville, Louisville, Birmingham, New York City, Miami, and Orlando.

She also walked the runway at the Waldorf Astoria in New York City and the Fountain Bleu in Miami as a plus-size model, where from both locations…she received various awards for modeling and acting competitions.

And, what convinced me to recruit her was the information given to me of her being a producer, writer, and director…and she held her producing and publishing copyrights (Mama'nem), (It's Our Time), and (Sistah-2-Sister) under the umbrella of G-Town Productions, LLC and BABS Publishing, LLC.

I was glad that I had contacted her to be a part of my production.

Finally, everything was working out with the cast I recruited for the play after a period.

We had a great turnout on August 13, 2016 in Gallatin, Tennessee.

My cousin Mary helped me out with bringing the food and sitting it up for the cast.

I told her she didn't have to bring anything, but she insisted on helping, anyway.

This is how people would bless me with their love in helping where they could.

When the cast walked in, you could tell by the surprised look on their face to have refreshments for the evening.

This is how I enjoy doing things though, plus I knew some of them had just come from work not having time to eat them something.

And, by doing this, I felt like we would have a better rehearsal with something on our stomach.

Even though we had some who came I was still short two cast members for the play.

When I was talking to Mary on the day at the festival there in Gallatin Tennessee, she saw two church members coming over to my table.

She said, "Now they might help you out in the play."

She introduced us and we started getting acquainted, when I asked them, "If they would like to be in my play?"

Minister Deborah Alston spoke up and said, "I think that I could do this."

Then she spoke up for Mr. Barr and said, "Baby, you can do it too." Right then is when we connected and we have been best friends ever since.

Within a minute or two they answered yes. I took their information down and told them I would call them with the time and place of the next rehearsal.

She even brought a couple of piece of the jewelry I was selling for the organization I was helping this friend of mines from Africa."

The money I raised was to help the women and children there in Africa with the special items they needed each month to take care of their care amongst other things.

Shortly afterward, I closed down the shop and started packing things up to go home.

I was thinking on the way home, now this makes the cast more complete.

Then it was time to search for another building to hold our plays when I used a place of my cousin.

Yes, again my cousin Mary stepped up to offer me to use a place that she had.

During the next week, everyone received a call we would start our weekly rehearsal.

On the day of rehearsal, I traveled to Gallatin, Tennessee to set up the food, chairs, and tables for the rehearsal.

We were lucky to have as many people come from Nashville, Tennessee; Russellville, Kentucky; Franklin, Kentucky; Gallatin, Tennessee; and Lebanon, Tennessee.

But most of all, I was glad to see Timothy Woodard come join us.

I was looking for a guy who stood six foot two inches tall, when I was given his name to call to see if he would be interested.

When I reached out to him to ask him to join us, he explained he was a little taller than that but he agreed anyway and took the leading role of Mr. Washington.

He was even able to help us pack the house on the night we had the play in Bowling Green, Kentucky with his family members and friends.

Later, I looked over at the door and in came Minister Deborah Alston and Mr. Terry Barr.

They were there on time like everyone else with the excitement of joining us in the play.

We had a meeting before we started about some things we needed for the play,

When Minister Deborah heard me talking about the things we needed for the play; she was kind enough to donate a few items to the company."

And so, did Bettie Britton who played Grandma Mattie. She gave more than her share of making sure I stayed afloat in this wonderful gift God gave me to share.

Her exact words were, "I have faith in you."

There were a few more cast members who donated whose names I cannot mention.

While working with them I notice something different from Betty Britton. She never missed a rehearsal.

Then it hit me…I could see by her being a producer, director, writer and professional actress in the industry and of her plays she knew how important it was to be at every rehearsal.

Some others missed a few rehearsals because of various reasons, but they still made it on stage.

If there weren't enough cast members for the show, I would be the one to bring up the rear.

I only added myself to the play only if it became necessary for me to step in.

I guess you can say that I was like one of the backup singers.

I was always ready and willing to fit myself in where I could.

This is what a director will do in times like these.

I became the understudy of many characters of these plays.

Ever since God revealed to me one day saying, who would better know these lines than you. You are at every rehearsal, and you are already learning the lines.

"Wow," I said, "God has a way of directing you in the direction he wants you to go."

I then said, "I didn't know I would act, but if you feel I can do this, God. I will step out on faith and try my best."

Since then…I've stepped out on faith and done this and I've become more confident in my journey.

While the cast and crew were all mingling with each other to get to know one another; we all became one big happy family.

As time went on, we all continued to bring food to eat; laughing, talking and having the best times while we were at rehearsal.

I had already made the deposit to hold the venue we looked at.

All I had to do was contact them to let them know the date of the play.

I called later and booked it for Friday, December 16, 2016.

On the day of the play, I could see how anxious the cast was about going on stage.

On that day we had an amazing crowd to show up.

The cast did an excellent job of acting that evening.

We came down off the stage afterward to mingle with the crowd when we heard so many compliments from the crowd on the cast performance.

This is when we started telling them there would be a Part II of "Grandma Mattie Gets Her a Man."

The people in the crowd were saying, "We are looking forward to seeing Part II of Grandma Mattie Gets Her a Man."

This was music to my ears to hear people talking about what a good time they had.

And the cast was excited about us doing the next show soon.

Then we all went next door where the reception party was being held at the Rico's Stage Lounge.

While the reception was going on, you could still hear the people talking about how much they enjoyed the play.

I was even happy to hear from the cast in how happy they were to be a part of the play.

This made me so happy to know I had once again been able to bless the people who came to see the play I had written with the creative writing skills God had given me.

Now since the play went so well in Gallatin, Tennessee; I took the play to Bowling Green, Kentucky and Franklin, Kentucky to a venue.

Once I told the cast we would travel, they were so excited to be traveling with the play.

So on January 22, 2017, we took the play to the Goodnight Library in Franklin, Kentucky.

Two cast members couldn't continue in the next play with us, so this is when I had to step in as understudy for their roll.

In being the producer and director, I had to learn quickly on how to cover the spaces when they became open.

This was the only way to keep things running smoothly.

My position stopped not only there.

I even went on the WBKO television show again on December 26, 2016, to promote the tickets for the next play.

But I stopped not only there…I went for my interview on the WRU radio station located in Russellville, Kentucky on December 30, 2016.

What touched my heart was to see my name up in the light for the play displayed up on a theater billboard in Bowling Green, Kentucky.

This was an amazing feeling like I had never felt before.

To know that people from all walks of life were passing this sign daily; seeing me up in lights just like the stars on television.

I could see my dream more and more coming true each time I took another step forward.

A lot of opportunities were unfolding right before my eyes and I couldn't believe it was real.

This is when I was wishing my parents were here to see what all I had accomplished.

People were leaving me messages on my page congratulating me, telling me how much they love the title, and my cousin Wanda Tuck said, "I told you, girl."

She was only confirming a conversation that we had some time ago about me progressing to a higher level.

Then it was time for us to be in Bowling Green, Kentucky on stage to give our performance of "Grandma Mattie Gets Her a Man."

Everyone was getting ready and taking their places on stage for the performance that night.

When I saw things were going on as planned then I took my position up in the sound room.

On tonight I went up in the sound room to watch the play. So that I could learn more about how my sound engineer Mr. Carlice Mockabee operated the soundboard.

This was in case he could not be with me for one of my plays.

I wanted to make sure I was up on everything going on in my production to make sure things run smoothly for my cast and the audience.

The youngest member of my staff was Lashanti Mockabee, who was the daughter of Mr. Carlice Mockabee.

She also worked in the sound room assisting her dad with the sound-board, making sure that he had everything that he needs.

While she was taking notes and learning what all she had to do.

She was planning on following in her father's footsteps to become a sound engineer too.

I was glad that I could give this youth a position in my production to have something to do and the older members of my staff.

I felt like giving the youth something to do would help keep them off the street corner.

Keeping our youth encouraged and out of trouble was part of my community duty, at least I thought.

Just like I tried to help them out when I started my Character Bus Company.

I started it because my daughter had nothing to do.

And when my daughter came to me and said, "I'm bored and there isn't anything to do."

I felt the need and my duty to give her something before someone else gave her something to do that would make me regret for the rest of my life.

This is when I saw the need to help the community in giving the children something to look forward to and keep them out of trouble.

Some parents could see the value of what I was doing, but some couldn't.

I let some kids ride free who wanted to go because they didn't have the funds.

There were things I tried to do in the community not accepted by many people, but I realize that everyone can't see what you see.

Many Blessings are being missed when this happens, all you can do is pray and keep it moving.

I've even given Christmas boxes to families for Christmas for years, brought some grocery for families when they called and said, "My family needs some food."

Knowing the mama was spending her money on drugs.

Many times I paid people rent who walked away from their responsibilities for years.

I've learned you can't always do what people want you to do.

You've got to do what God is leading you to do.

What some people cannot realize God gave us all a vision to use our vision to the best of our ability even if it's not what others want us to do.

And I've learned why God has chosen people to step in to help you while he is guiding you along the way.

For them to have and to hold you up while you are on this tedious journey.

All you have to do is stop listen and learn to obey the words his sending you.

Those people will show up and show out right on time.

Many people are happy for me, they have been following me from the first day I started my journey which gives me such great joy and happiness.

Again, God has allowed me to come through with the gift he has given me to use.

Not only did I stop there, I wrote Part II of "Grandma Mattie Gets Her a Man."

By now, I was feeling more comfortable in writing and traveling with my extraordinary plays, with the ambition of taking on more cast for my plays.

The confidence I was having had led me to travel more with my plays.

On March 4, 2017, we took the play to 301 Bunche Avenue in Glasgow, Kentucky.

Here is where I met a very nice young lady, her daughter, and mother, who came to Bowling Green, Kentucky to attend my book signing event which you will hear about later on in this story.

It was good to see I had touched their lives in such a-way they wanted to share this day with me and purchase a book.

The power of God is real when we are obedient to his word.

On February 27, 2017, I traveled to Chattanooga, Tennessee to meet with the Stage Director of the Chattanooga State Community College

Here is where one of my cast members took me to meet Mr. Charles Patterson.

He is a Chattanooga native…a twenty-seven-year veteran of the Chattanooga Fire Department where he held the rank of Captain before he retired in 2017.

He is also a Writer, Producer, and Director of Christal Entertainment Productions (CEP).

Charles has a passion for political debates, sports, theater and film.

Growing up watching his favorite football team, the Pittsburgh Steelers, he immediately became impressed with their dominating presence and how accurate and precise the Steelers executed their plays on both defense and offense.

With that being said, Charles has adapted that same principle in directing his stage productions; tough and in your face.

Over the past several years in the Chattanooga area, Charles' productions have been about life's complexities and have raised some eyebrows.

Charles is committed to enhancing the hidden talent of actors while creating a vehicle for cultural enrichment, education, creative stimulation, spiritual inspiration, and just good old family laughter that has you coming back for more.

He is motivated and passionate about incorporating social issues of today into his theatrical productions.

Charles carries a thankful but humble heart for his God-given talent, and states, "Acting is an art, and is best when it imitates real-life situation."

Some of his resume comprise: "The First Lady," "Choices," "God Said It," (Film); "He's A Good Man," "No Man Can Stop You," "Home Going–Tiny Jenkins," "Sahkanaga" (Film); "Twelve Angry Jurors," "A New Beginning," "Stand Up for Freedom," "Christmas Thieves,"… and many more credits not listed dating back to 1992.

Charles is married with three children and attends Orchard Knob Missionary Baptist Church.

Charles believes whatever you go through is for a reason; to come out stronger than before while giving God all the glory.

He has always expressed his sincere gratitude to the Chattanooga community for their continued support.

Charles truly believes what God has for you, is for you… claim it!

We became acquainted and shared information to collaborate on my play that I was planning on bringing to the area soon.

He suggested a few of the Venues where I could have my play.

While talking I asked, "Would you be interested in being a cast member in my play?"

He smiled, within a few minutes he agreed to take apart in the play. Then we exchanged phone numbers so we could keep in touch with one another.

Believe this or not, I had spoken these exact words to my cast just a little while ago. We would start traveling on tour.

The time was gradually beginning to come around sooner than I had realized.

God was moving at me with a fast pace, and I was ready, willing, to carry out what he had given me to do.

Thank you, God, for everything you have done in our lives to fulfill this opportunity that you have given me and my cast. You are worthy to have all the glory and praise.

Meanwhile, on April 2, 2017, I gave my cast members dinner. We had a photo-shoot that day for our new flyer.

I asked everyone to wear white outfits for the pictures.

They did and all of them looked amazing; we had a great time socializing then we had our rehearsal.

On April 22, 2017, some of my cast attended the Franklin-Simpson Human Rights Commission, Unsung Heroes Banquet with me.

My heart went out to these amazing people for being such a great hero in our community.

I was glad to be there on the day to witness and share this special event with them.

When the weeks and days went by, I was feeling like I needed a vacation from all the running I had been doing.

So on July 4, 2017, I started contacting family members to see if they wanted to travel to Saint Louis, Missouri in August.

I figured this would be a great place for the kids to go to the zoo.

Some replied, and some didn't, but at least I would be with my family soon.

Now it was time for me to travel to Chattanooga, Tennessee on June 11, 2017, to check in my room at the hotel to get some rest for the big day.

On the next day of June 12, 2017, I was going on the community news Fox channel to have an interview with Mr. Greg Funderburg.

In meeting Mr. Greg Funderburg, I have been able to keep in touch with him through text and emails, sharing more of my creative writing journey with him.

He then told me he would be glad to share this information with his family and friends.

Since then I've also been able to go back to the show to talk on, "This N That" there at the station, which you will hear about later on in my story.

When I go back to look at the trailer I made from my interview with Mr. Greg Funderburg. I saw over one thousand, four hundred ninety-two views.

This brought a smile to my face to see these many people were curious to see what was going on with me.

I also notice I had over a thousand followers taking an interest in my journey.

What an amazing feeling to know that I had come a long way to get to this point in my life.

Most of all, it was great to see and hear some comments made by some of my home-girls.

Jane Lewis - Sarah Tuck… You are a Force!!! Praying God continues to pour out his blessing on you.

Wanda Tuck-CONGRATULATIONS CUZ, so proud of you and your accomplishments, watch out Broadway, New York, New York.

Mary Spencer-CONGRATULATIONS TO YOU AND MUCH SUCCESS IN THE FUTURE!

Myra Tuck Tarrence - My prayers are with you sister-in-law continue to let God be the head.

This was only a portion of what was being said.

There were so many more messages left for me till I just can't tell it all.

These people were seeing the same force of God working with me I was seeing.

4

STARTED WRITING MY FIRST BOOK

We had prepared ourselves in rehearsal for our trip to Louisville, Kentucky for our next performance.

I thought of contacting the radio station at WLOU there in Louisville, Kentucky to promote my play.

When I did, they agreed to let me come on the show and I felt like I did a fantastic job.

When I heard it later, I knew that I had accomplished another task to put under my belt.

On July 15, 2017, it was time to travel back to Louisville, Kentucky, to the "Eastern Star Baptist Church Family Life Center."

We were short-handed tonight because I had someone to drop out eight days before the play.

But I prayed about it. Then we pulled it together to make it work, anyway.

It was something about tonight though I felt it would be special because this was the night that we filmed and made our first trailer.

Yes, it was finally happening, we had made our first trailer from the play, "Grandma Mattie Gets Her a Man."

Then later I had it added to Vimeo and YouTube, then put on my site for the world to see.

It was amazing to see the next step I had accomplished with my creative writing.

This couldn't have been possible if we had not all pulled together on this day to help make this trailer come through.

I was seeing God taking me to another level in my adventure of Sarah Tuck Creative Writing.

It was plain as the writing on the wall.

HE JUST KEEPS ON BLESSING ME!

I remembered having compliments like "Love It, Love it very exciting…God Bless, It's wonderful, Nice."

As time went on, I wind up with having over 600 views for this trailer.

I'm sure there have been even more views since then.

Many things were taking place through my journey, as you can see.

And all I continued to do is ask God to continue to give me the room to accept what you have for me next.

It was time for the annual weekend Festival in Russellville, Kentucky.

I took some time off to support some friends and family there in Russellville, Kentucky.

On August 5, 2017, I traveled to the Annual Event in Russellville, Kentucky just as I have frequently.

While I was there, I ran into a Producer who showed us her film of "Cooper's Plantation."

At that very moment, it filled me with confirmation on what I had done in making my first trailer.

I felt like God was showing me I was on the right track, to stay steady fast forward on there are greater things to come.

Seeing this gave me such great confirmation in knowing I had finally accomplished another goal.

I have kept in touch with this writer from time to time, following her in her Creative Writing and filming. I see how she is making waves in her community and around the world.

Still motivated and eager, I then recruited the cast for Part II of, "Grandma Mattie Gets Her a Man."

The lady named Betty Britton who played the character of Grandma Mattie wasn't able to continue with us due to various reasons.

She told me she would be back when she could come back.

I was so glad to hear this.

Meanwhile, it was time to take a short trip with the family and go to Saint Louis, Missouri to have a little family fun.

I had planned this back in July when I realized I needed to take some time off.

We traveled there, and I stayed three nights, then came back to finish getting ready for the play.

When I came back…I started searching for another person to play the lead role when I was told to contact a lady in Louisville, Kentucky. We met, and she had her audition in August 2017.

I recruited her, and a few more cast members when I held more various rehearsals getting ready for our performance for the play.

Meanwhile, it was getting into August 2018 when I was having thoughts of writing my first book.

So, within two days I sat down at the computer and started gathering my material from my play of "Grandma Mattie Gets Her a Man."

In preparing to start my book I just started typing and looking over my script then typing more.

Till suddenly I had my first chapter already written.

I was sitting there looking at what I had written and started thinking of how I would start the next chapter.

Thereafter, I started on the second chapter soon afterwards I saw I had finished.

This is when I felt I needed to take a break.

Each day or two after that I continued to write and read back over what I had written.

Then I could see it was coming true for me I was finally writing a book for the first time.

When I started looking at the photo's seeing which one I would use for the cover.

Then I choose the one I wanted to use.

So, I texted Betty and asked her if I could use her picture to put on the front cover of my book.

I said, "I'm going to step out on faith to see how this goes."

Within a few minutes, she was texted me backing saying, "Yes."

I replied, "Great."

Then I told her, "I was talking with some publishing companies trying to see which ones were the best."

"I feel good about this decision. I've been praying off and on for a while now."

She said, "Okey-Dokey."

She was always willing to help me…whenever I needed her…she was there.

Plus, she knew how hard of a time I was having getting to where I was today.

I had called to ask this person about the publishing company they were using for their book.

I wanted to see if this was a good company to publish my book with.

Only to get turned away by saying, "Oh, I'm so busy right now with getting our pastor's annual day together. I will call you back next week."

Well, guess what, next week never came around.

Then I contacted another lady that had finished her book. She was always busy, and she too told me she would contact me later.

But she never did. This didn't stop me though; instead it gave me more motivation to continue to keep on pushing till I found the answers I was looking for.

People need to realize if you don't help me, I'm just going to go where someone will.

There is enough room for all of us and I will take the extra mile to go where I need to go to get what I need.

So, I contacted the producer of "Cooper's Plantation."

She was more than willing to help me with the information I needed.

As I've said before, God has certain people that will help you when you are on your journey.

You just have to trust and believe and continue to pray.

A while after this I got together with the cast on having a fish fry to help raise money for the expenses we had.

We had the fish fry on August 26, 2017, therein Gallatin, Tennessee.

It wasn't as successful as I would have liked for it to have been.

But they blessed us with what they gave us that day.

Later, I held my first Gospel Fest in Bowling Green, Kentucky on September 30, 2017. I started contacting some of my cast then they gave me other contacts…who I contacted and asked to perform for me."

But before having the Gospel Fest, I traveled to Atlanta, Georgia to meet with a High School friend on September 2, 2017, named Paula Sweeney.

We had been collaborating on the phone about me bringing my play to Atlanta, Georgia sometimes.

We had dinner on that Saturday evening. Then I went over to her house to catch up on some social time.

Then we departed saying our goodnights. Then I headed to the motel to get some sleep.

The next day I got up, getting ready so I could attend church with her.

While I was worshipping with her, it blessed me to see my friend and her husband Minister Greg Sweeney & Minister Paula Key Sweeney working side by side in their community.

She had told me once before she was a Minister a while back, but to see her up there praying and doing God's work blessed my soul.

Again, I was glad to be surrounding myself with other spiritual people who I could attend church with while I was away from my church home.

On September 26, 2017, I went back to WBKO, this time to promote my Gospel Fest.

Then once again I was on WRUS radio station live in Russellville, Kentucky having my interview about the Gospel Fest there.

I was moving right along when one day I was checking on my website and notice that some of my friends had left me a note saying someone had sent them another friend request from me.

It displeased me in what I had read, then I wrote a message on my page telling everyone that it wasn't me sending the message and to please don't except another friend's request.

Knowing how people say things on your site to make you look bad was a thought I didn't want to have.

Then I wrote: We live in a world today where people should love one another and treating each day like it was our last day. God is showing us through the flood in Texas and the tornado that happened a few days ago.

Instead, some of them would rather do harm to people thinking they will never have to pay. Judgment day is a day that we all will have to stand before God for all of our wrongdoings.

So, I'm praying for you right now because you're lost. I pray that you find God almighty before this day comes. Cry out to God, for you need him now.

When I got over that, I then traveled to South Carolina to Myrtle Beach with some of my cast members for the wedding.

Yes, I could finally take pictures of the wedding of two of my cast members to put in my play.

I had asked this couple some time ago could I put this in my play when I found out they were getting married.

Using this wedding around my story was such a great honor, and I was pleased to be doing this with them.

I was so glad they allowed me to use their wedding in my play and being a part of it.

I named this play "Uncle Jessie & Aunt Pauline Wedding Day."

Moving right along, it was time to hold the Gospel Fest on September 30, 2017.

There were guests who came to sing from, "Louisville, Kentucky, Bowling Green, Kentucky and Gallatin, Tennessee."

It turned out to be an Awesome Gospel Fest…the people loved it and stated they would like to attend another one if I had one.

Some compliments were: Superb! May God Bless you in everything that you do! May God continue to bless you and your vision for bringing life to your plays.

Felicia Bland admired my determination of being obedient to God for the calling of the assignment God had for me.

She was always in the mix with me from time to time, watching and listening to what God was having me to deliver to the people.

Minister Darren Bush was there…along with a few of my other casts.

Then on October 4, 2017, I traveled back to Gallatin, Tennessee, to the Palace Theatre to book the place for my new play "Grandma Mattie Goes to Church."

As I went back to my car, I was thinking about how far I had come.

I had to take a moment to give praises to God for letting me still being here to do his will.

So, when I went home, I sat down at the computer and wrote this.

Those of you know that three years ago God gave me a gift to use for his good. I promised to be obedient and follow through with it. Now, I've planted the seed God gave me by the people he put into my life and removed from my life.

People speak to me and others have shown me the seed I sowed. I can see this on people's faces, through their messages, phone calls prayer, by bringing the gift of love, and going out of the way to help me plant the seed. God is not through with me yet.

I added this to my page to share with the world how God is still working with me.

I then continued making all the arrangements after I completed them I could have the play on October 28, 2017, at the Palace Theater in Gallatin, Tennessee.

My work was being seen by the other producer who wanted to work with me.

Then in November 2017, I was asked to join another writer and producer named Michael Cantrell in being his assistant director in his play "Horror Movie 101."

He had asked me if I would be Co.-Director with him on this play with his cast members.

I've always wanted to work with the other producer to see how they operated.

We had our first rehearsal in Bowling Green, Kentucky at the Western Kentucky University Downing Center.

After several weeks of rehearsal, the time had come for us to hold our first show on January 7, 2018.

The play was a success, and the audience loved it.

On December 2, 2017, they invited me to a special Gospel Event in Louisville, Kentucky where I met this amazing artist named Mrs. Jacqueline Smith.

We kept in touch then I asked her to come to sing in one of my plays that you will hear about later on in my story.

Oh…but, before the play took place on December 11, 2017, I wrote about a give-a-way on my Social page for the first five people to contact me and they would receive a DVD of "Grandma Mattie Gets Her a Man."

This is when I became acquainted with Minister Roy Bell.

He was one winner for one of my free DVD.

When he called me, I was on the phone at the present time. So, I had to call him back to let him know that he had won.

We talked for a while then I got off the phone.

I went back on the site and was scrolling down when I saw were Minister Roy Bell was having an open conversation with a lady I used to ride the bus with…talking about me.

I could tell by what I saw he couldn't have been on the site that long.

He should have been talking in messenger. But instead, he was placing the message on his wall for everyone to see.

Unless he didn't care who knew what he was saying.

And, if you know him as I do now, he didn't care.

Anyway, he asked her if she knew me. Her response was, "All our lives. We went to school together."

He said, "Great." She wrote "Laugh-out-loud. Nice Lady."

He replied, "Really Lady material, girlfriend material or wife material."

She then wrote a question mark. He then said, "Ok, I met her while I was answering her give-away Ad on social media, we've had a great conversation today for about two hours. "I'm impressed…you know me I don't impress easy…I'd like to get to know her better I trust your judgment."

She came back with, "Nice lady. And, you will…LOL." He then wrote a question mark then said, "I will be oooooookkk."I was shocked.

5

TRAVELED TO BOWLING GREEN, KENTUCKY FOR THE NEXT PLAY

My next step was to travel to Bowling Green, Kentucky, to recruit my fourth set of cast members for the play called "Ray Jay Senior Year."

But before I went there to make this project happen, I wanted to explore some other options to see what I could come up with.

I put out an Ad to hold an Audition for more cast members, stagehands, and musicians as well as singers.

As usual, I didn't have anyone that wanted to come aboard to join us.

So, I continue to go ahead with my plans of working with someone in Bowling Green to see what we could come up with.

We came together and talked about him asking some cast members that he had worked with to come out for the audition that I had set up.

It blessed me to have all the cast members that came out to join us after they made the audition in 2018.

These cast members were in a revolving production that had played off and on throughout the year.

Let me explain what I mean by this. Some of them came to be in my play while they were already in another play or were waiting to hear if they got the part in another one.

I wasn't too fond of this situation because, I didn't see how they could dedicate themselves to my play, and then be in another at the same time.

However, the gentleman who I will call Mike made the statement that they do this all the time.

So I proceeded on with the recruiting, then I started the rehearsals.

Then after we had a few rehearsals, I started getting messages that some cast couldn't come to rehearsal.

I knew right then this was a bad idea.

One person called out almost every time I had a rehearsal for the first two to three times.

I already knew that this would happen.

Yes, you can't be in two places at the same time. Therefore, I was in hesitation in taking on some of them.

I wanted to give them an opportunity I thought to be in my production so I recruit them, anyway.

Word of advice, if someone gives you an opportunity then you should try to give it your best shot.

Later on, I could see they were not as interested in the play as I had once seen them in the beginning.

I feel like it was because they were trying to burn the candle at both ends.

And when I let one of them go then recruit someone else.

He couldn't see that he had done anything wrong.

But, as I tell all of my cast members, you can't teach someone if they don't come to rehearsal.

The other people are trying to learn, cannot learn their lines if the other person is not there to say their lines.

Therefore I set up a rehearsal schedule so everyone can come and say their line.

When you cannot come to do this, then I have to keep filling in for you, and it's not fair to me or the other cast members.

Especially, when you have lines to learn and so do I too.

I didn't mind hearing some suggestions on some things, but; I felt like a few people were trying to run things.

It was hard to make them understand that God gave me the vision and not them.

I don't mean this in a smart or nasty way, but I just needed people to work with me on what I have to offer them so that they could see the bigger picture later, so they can be a part of it as well.

Many didn't wait to see what would happen, some bale before the next show after they had promised to be in the next show.

Not thinking this would go on file.

And, if another producer asked me about you, I would have to tell them the truth.

We then took the play to Louisville, Kentucky…where we had a fairly good turnout. Meanwhile, I was preparing for a trip to Atlanta to attend a "Women's Red-Carpet Event."

When Ms. Wanda Tuck contacted me a week before I was leaving asking me if I could attend their Women's History Month.

She said, "You had won an award from the Franklin Simpson Human Rights Commission."

The name of this award was for "Celebration of Women History Month."

This award was for some women who had achieved the movement of doing things in the community. I explained that I would be out of town during this time and I had already made my reservation.

So, on my way back from attending another women's celebration in Atlanta, Georgia.

I stopped by Wanda Tuck's house to receive my Award.

All I could say was, "God Keeps On Blessing Me."

Again, I was being recognized for the great works that I had done in the community by this organization who gave me a helping hand when I first started my creative writing journey.

And I will never forget what they have done for me.

It was nice of them to consider me as one of the candidates with the other ladies that were nominated on this day.

I'm sure that they were just as excited as I was on this day.

I appreciated this day to the highest and I'm sure we all will remember it.

I couldn't wait to go home to share this exciting news with my daughter.

On March 24, 2018, my cousin invited me to her, 2018 IGNITE Women's Retreat & Expo, in Gallatin Tennessee.

She wanted me to come as a vendor.

I was glad that she had chosen me to take part because I needed the exposure for my production company.

It was an honor to be there to see her accomplishment she had made with the IGNITE Women's Retreat & Expo.

While I was there, I meant a lot of other vendors.

It blessed me in meeting many other vendors, getting contact to invite them to some of my functions.

This gave me the opportunity to exchange my information with them, and they did the same.

I was already planning on calling them to help me out with one of my functions.

On Saturday, April 28, 2018, I left Franklin, Kentucky going to Nashville, Tennessee to pick up one of my home-girls named Paula, who was traveling in from Atlanta, Georgia.

As soon as, I picked her up we headed to Memphis, Tennessee to see if I could find a venue to hold my play there.

When we arrived, we checked in, then we picked up something to eat. I made a few phone calls to a friend and was able to set an appointment for Monday, April 30, 2018.

On that day Paula and I had attended church there on the next day.

So, we started looking up the different churches to go to.

When one of my other girlfriends named Mary had called me or either I called her and while we were talking and I was telling her I was trying to find a church to attend.

She suggested that we attend the Temple of Deliverance she had gone there several times when she was in town then she said, "I think this will be a great church to attend."

When I got off the phone "I shared the information with Paula, she agreed then we got dressed to go out shopping then we headed back to the room."

I asked her if she wanted to do anything that night and she said, "No she didn't want to go anywhere so we stayed in our room watched television till we both fell asleep."

On Sunday morning, April 29, 2018, we both got up. "I went down for breakfast because Paula wasn't a breakfast eater that much."

Then I came back up to the room and started getting ready for church.

Soon after we dressed, I said, "Let's take some pictures" And we did, then I convinced her to make a short video to promote my play."

When we finished doing this, we went downstairs got into the van. Then I drove us over to where the church then parked. We got out of the van and headed to the front door of the church.

While we entered inside, there were some ushers standing close to the door along with more people that greeted us with their smiles and handshake.

Then we proceeded into the sanctuary of the church and took our seats while we were looking around at the size of the church the choir came in you should have seen this choir it was a large choir with a lot of talent singers in it.

I then happen to be looking to my left when I saw the usher heading my way with someone.

It surprised me to see her seat the young man in the vacant seat right beside me. "I looked around to see a lot of other available seats where he could have sat.

Instead, he had to sit down in the empty seat right beside me. Yes, I was a little uncomfortable because I didn't have much elbow room.

Then is when I asked myself why, did he have to set in the seat beside me when there were a lot of other seats in here.

You know me being the person I am turned to smile at him then I spoke to him and he had spoken back. Then I said, "Um…he's not a bad-looking guy." Then I asked God, "Are you trying to tell me something?" Then I smiled and didn't think much more of it.

You know here lately, I have often wondered if he had noticed me when I came into the building, then watched me take my seat.

Only God knows if that was the case or not. And, if it was, I don't think he would ever reveal it to me because of his pride.

I wanted to get up and move but that would have been rude for us to get up and move so we continued to sit there waiting for the service to start.

Shortly afterward, the services started. There were some spiritual dancers that came out on stage to perform for us.

They were a group of men wearing white paint on their faces with white gloves and they all wore black attire.

I don't remember the exact song that they used for the spiritual dance but, I really enjoyed it.

I then turned to the guy sitting next to me and explained to him I would love to have them open up for me when I brought my show here.

He then started inquiring, asking me, "What do you do?"

Then I explained to him I was a writer, producer and director of my plays.

He then spoke up and said, "It wouldn't be a problem to get them to perform for you. I could arranged for them to do this for you," then he asked me if he could have a card.

I said, "Yes," and reached into my purse and pulled out a card to give him. He smiled looked at it then he put it in his jacket as we continue listening to the service.

Their performance was amazing to see.

Shortly after the service was over Paula and I went back to the room to change.

Meanwhile, got something to eat then we wind up staying in for the rest of the night watching television again going to sleep.

On Monday morning we got up, getting ready to leave to go over to meet with the lady to see the venue.

When we left there, we stopped gas up and headed to Atlanta, Georgia to take Paula back home.

It was a long ride there but thank God we made it safely there where I spent the night with her and her husband before heading back home.

6

HONORED FOR THE STRATHMORE'S WHO'S WHO BOOK

I was sitting at home one day relaxing when the phone rang.
I received a call from a very nice lady telling me she was from the Strathmore's Who's Who.

She introduced herself and then started asking me questions about my play and even more.

Like what made me want to write and what inspired me to write plays.

I started telling her what, was at the tip of my tongue in how I got started and what encouragement me to write.

When we finished talking…her exact words were, "Congratulations we have accepted you into the book of Strathmore's Who's Who."

Well, as you could imagine, I was sitting there with my mouth open in disbelief that this was happening to me.

Just for taking out a few minutes to talk to someone about my creative writing.

Oh, I was so excited, I couldn't wait to get off the phone and I told a few people.

Then one day in the early month of July 2018, I received my certificate of honor.

I couldn't wait to share it with everyone.

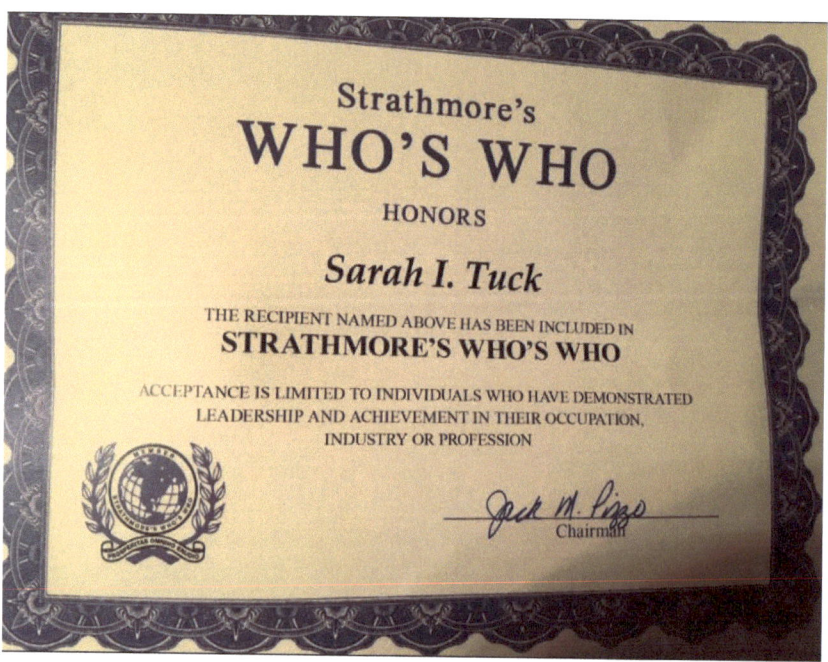

But before I started sharing my certificate with the world, we had the play of Ray Jay's Senior Year in Bowling Green, Kentucky.

I was already having some difficulties with some cast before the play.

So, I hoped that on the day of the play we could get through this day without any more issues.

I even cooked food for the cast on this day to make sure they had a good meal to eat before going on stage."

When suddenly I was hearing and seeing things I couldn't believe that was happening.

One of the cast members bought another person behind the stage without asking first.

I felt like this was rude and out of order because if the building had caught on fire, and I didn't know she was in there, she could have gotten left in the building and burned up.

Sometimes people do things without thinking about the consequences that could occur later.

When I asked who was this person, and where are they going?

I was told with a smart attitude she is with me, and she is helping me change.

When I walked over to ask Mark, "Did you give her the permission for this person to be in the back of the stage?"

He replied, "No, we all got dressed the other day without help."

I then said, "That's just what I thought. I didn't think she should have been back there."

I could see that things were getting out of hand.

I knew right then that some cast was having problems with following the rules.

Then later on one of the other cast members came out and asked me if it was ok if the young girl could stay backstage with them.

I appreciated her coming to me without asking. I felt like this person knew that it was wrong for them not to ask permission, so she felt like doing the right thing.

So we proceeded right along with having the performance.

I was pleased to have a few vendors with us on this day.

We had one with scented candles, Tupperware, paparazzi jewelry and my DVD's.

There were some that didn't get to make it due to things that came up preventing them to come.

However, it was a blessing and honored to have Pastor Jacqueline Smith to come to be a part of my play by singing one of her songs, "A God Kind of Love."

She is an Ordained Pastor, Prophetic Teacher/Seer, Prophet Psalmist, Artist, Author, Women's Advocate/Women's Empowerment.

She also is the Founder at AWE Anointed Women Empowered and she is a Music Artist.

It was a blessing to have her join us and hear her on tonight. She said, "She was blessed by what she had just witnessed."

And she could see God doing amazing things in my ministry.

Then, after the play was over, the people gave their compliments and took pictures with us.

Now by being in the play, I wasn't able to see what everyone had on until I saw the film that I paid for being filmed.

Betty Ann Britton, my photographer, made the film then gave it to me to sit down to watch. I was very disappointed in what I was watching.

One of the cast members had worn some shorts that were too short and I wasn't able to use the film.

From then on, I learned that some rules had to be set in order for this not to happen again.

Even other things took place that I was unhappy about.

Later I talked to Mark to let him know all the things I saw go wrong.

I made some changes so this wouldn't happen again.

Later I was talking to Minister Bell about how displeased I was in some things that had occurred. He then offered to be my manager to help me with some problems I was having with my cast.

Then I agreed and took him up on his offer.

I traveled on July 7, 2018, to Louisville, Kentucky for my first time of being at the Better Days West End record store.

The owner, Mr. Ben Jones gave me permission to set up my display outside the store by the front entrance to promote my play.

He was such a nice man; he even told me that I could come back anytime I needed to come. His door was always open.

Hearing this statement coming from him made me feel like there was another new beginning forming and shaping in my journey.

This was a great feeling and honor to be sitting by the door of this record store talking to the people as they were going in or coming out.

I could share my information with them about us bringing the play to town and letting them watch a trailer of one of my plays.

This was awesome to see another door had opened for me.

There were drawings for door prizes on that day for tickets for the play and some DVD's selling.

When I had some free time, I wrote the play of Part II, Ray Jay's Senior Year.

Then on August 1, 2018, I had finished writing this play.

Once again, I had conquered my goal of what I had sat out to do.

I was moving right along because I had to go back on the road again to Louisville, Kentucky.

I had met with a lady a while back that was telling me about a women's retreat in Louisville, Kentucky.

So, I looked up the information on attending it sometime soon.

But, little did I know they had an opening for me on August 12, 2018.

Yes, I went there on Sunday and stayed there till the following Sunday morning by myself.

There was a mix-up in the booking that week so I had to stay in this big place all by myself.

This really wasn't bad because while I was there, I could write an entire script of Part II "Ray Jay's Senior Year."

By this place, being quiet and secluded gave me the opportunity to concentrate on everything I needed to make this play a hit.

I then thought about recruiting more cast members, to help with the new plays that I had written.

I had received some referrals from some of the cast members then followed upon them.

I was traveling back and forth to Louisville, Kentucky to hold rehearsals with them trying to get them ready for the play.

I traveled to Louisville, Kentucky to attend the Greater Friendship Baptist Church to worship with a friend.

Then shortly after services, I meant with the lady over the booking of the building where I was planning on having my play.

This building was right next door to the church, it was their fellowship hall.

We completed the paperwork then we talked about future engagements.

I went back home after the weekend was over to continue holding rehearsal for the play on July 28, 2018.

This play would take place this time in Louisville at the Greater Friendship Church.

It was time for Minister Roy Bell to discuss with me officially becoming my manager on July, 31, 2018.

He is a native of Cross Plains, Tennessee, where he lives.

He has two sons and three great-grandchildren that he is very proud of.

He started in my production as a narrator, after which he volunteered to become the manager.

Since he was interested in becoming the manager we sat down and discussed this matter, then we finally came to a mutual agreement.

We bonded this agreement between the two of us when he said, "As long as he didn't have to deal with the recruiting of the cast members or deal with the money."

He wanted to leave these two things up to me and the board members.

Then we made plans to travel to Louisville, Kentucky on September 8, 2018, for our next rehearsal.

On that day, Mr. Bennett Gatewood traveled with us there.

This is when I saw my manager, Minister Roy Bell, filling in by taking one characters role to help the young man who came in from Louisville to help him learn his lines.

Seeing him do this gave me a sense of unity, of having him with my staff and me.

Also, I felt like he was being a good example and role model for the staff and the youth of this production.

Even the young man was showing us he is willing to listen, and follow instructions to become what he needed to be on the stage.

We had rehearsals again, getting ready for our play when a few weren't showing up again.

This is when I called Minister Roy Bell to let him know again this was not acceptable.

During our conversation, he shouted at me. I politely said, "Good-Bye."

I felt like he had something going on with him to talk to me like this.

So, we didn't talk for a while till he came to realize this is not the way you conduct business with me.

From that day forward he said, "I'm at a better place now" and basically, he was apologizing for what he had done.

I realized that we all are under pressure from time to time, but we have to learn to control our emotions.

Since then we have learned to conduct business and get along better than we once did.

On September 22, 2018, we took the play to Franklin, Kentucky again, to the Cornerstone at Franklin Presbyterian Church.

The day didn't start out the way I would have liked it too.

I was getting calls two hours before the play about many things.

Not to mention on this day I locked my keys in my van where the props were.

I had to wait over an hour and a half for someone to bring me a key.

Then on top of this I faced one of my cast members not showing.

I asked two cast members to cover his scenes, and they did.

We were finally ready to perform when I looked out in the audience and saw a small crowd.

I thought my hometown had let us down again, but later I learned that one of the reason was there were two other events going on this day.

We came out anyway and by the grace of God the four of us carried out the performance as if all the cast were present.

The ones that came through enjoyed the play and were proud they came.

I was glad to see my former Sunday school teacher there, Mrs. Alice Bailey. She was always there, supporting me whenever she could.

I even had four classmates to show up on that day to see the performance.

Two of them were actually helping me on that day.

Well believe it or not I had to start travel again, it seemed like I was doing a lot of this along this journey.

On October 6, 2018, it was time to travel to Louisville, Kentucky to promote the play of "Ray Jay's Senior Year."

Shortly after I went there and had set up when I looked around and here came in Pastor Jacqueline Smith.

She was there on this day to help promote the play too.

I had asked her to come to join me so the people could meet the person who would sing at our next play.

While she was there, we were selling the CD of her latest hits and the DVD of my former play of "Grandma Mattie Gets Her a Man."

Soon afterward on October 27, 2018, they invited me to attend the Kiwanis Club of Franklin Simpson for their Twelve-year anniversary celebration.

They gave me an invitation to join, but due to my commitment to my production and writing company, I didn't have room and time to become a member.

But, I offered to help them whenever I could be of help to them if they needed me.

Then in late December 2018, I placed a post-up on my site saying; "Well, it's been four-half-years I've been on my journey, with my production company. While I've been on this journey, I wanted to give thanks to all of my cast members who have been faithful, attending, and who has stuck by me through thick and thin who wanted to see me accomplish what I have accomplished."

Looking back, I know God had to be the one leading and guiding me on this journey every day.

The time had come for me to give honor to one of our cast members that had been faithful in all she could do to help me.

Mrs. Betty Ann Britton was given recognition for me nominating her for the new position of becoming my assistant director, videographer, and photographer.

During the month of February, as we all know, we celebrate "Black History Month."

This is when we as people and especially black people…celebrate the history of people who have accomplished great things to help pave the way for others.

Now I can proudly say that I am a part of the black history…we will be celebrated from now on.

I want to take the time to give thanks to the Franklin-Simpson Human Rights Commission for adding me in their write up on February 5, 2019.

<u>*This is what they felt like writing up on me:*</u>

Franklin-Simpson Human Rights Commission

HONORING BLACK HISTORY MONTH

Sarah Irene, Tuck

Sarah is a writer, producer, director and actor of her own production company, "Sarah Tuck Production".

She is an entrepreneur, still rising up in the different fields of opportunities that become available to her to help her reach out and grasp a hold of whatever God gives her to make these dreams come true.

She started her writing experience many, many years ago, but God revealed to her in May 2014, it's your time to step out.

Sarah plays consist of: "Shantel Leaves the Nest," "Grandma Mattie Gets Her a Man I & II," "My Son is Coming Home," "Ray Jay's Senior Year."

She has presented each play as a stage production and film.

She will soon release her first book.

This was indeed an honor to be making history.

While still here to celebrate Black History.

Well, it was getting closer to time to finish my book.

I was back and forth with my editor and the person who was making my cover for the book.

While waiting for another week or two for everything to come through.

I was patiently sitting there waiting for my book to come through the computer.

When suddenly it happened I was looking at my book this brought tears to my eyes.

I cried for two whole days after seeing my book.

I was still in wonderland wondering could this be true.

You had to see it in order to believe this was my first book.

And now I was excited about writing my second one.

But before I did, I pushed the button and waited for the final results for officially having my book completed.

Then I looked on Amazon.com and there it was I was proud once again for God giving me the chance to do his will.

7

ATTENDING MY FIRST BOOK SIGNING

In this chapter, you will see when I became an Author. I then checked on some places to have my book signing…when I was advised to call Ms. Lisa Deavers at the Gallery on the Square here in Franklin, Kentucky.

My call was successful. So, the next thing I did was make some flyers and I started sending out emails and text letting people know I was having a book signing.

I even put it in the newspaper of the Franklin Favorite.

Many people had to express how glad they would be to be purchasing my book.

Then I made some calls and had some friends to donate me some refreshments for my book signing.

On Saturday, February 9, 2019; I headed downtown to the Gallery on the Square for the "big day"

I had family and friends to show up and even people I didn't know.

Left to right with myself: Ms. Norma Flippin, Ms. Charlotte Detherage, Ms. Tammy McDonald, and Carmen Burnam.

We socialized ate, and I signed the books they purchased.

My nephew Jonathan Ford came and took the photo you will see in this story.

He also fixed me a short video to put up, so the viewers and fans could watch on my site.

I will never forget the last lady that came through the door.

She said, "I'm here to get me a book, I want to find out how Grandma Mattie was getting her a man; because if she can get one, I think I can get one."

Everyone started laughing at hearing her say this.

I told her she was just in time I had one left.

Yes…I sold out on that day and was so happy.

Oh, and one of my friends from way back named, Inita Rippy contacted me to let me know she wanted a book. She lived in Virginia Beach, Virginia.

I texted her back and asked her for her address then I sent her one. She wanted her book signed.

Over the year she has purchased all 5 books and was so kind as to send me a picture of them lying on her table.

She was always bragging on how good the books were and she wanted me to keep on writing.

Since she had posted this up on her social media site, I thought it would be nice to add her to the cover of my book.

When I called her to ask her if this would be alright, she responded with sure this would be fine with her.

I'm glad we are still friends and she is still continuing to support me in my endeavors.

I had been collaborating with my cousin Ms. Marilyn Strong who had to messenger me back on January 05, 2018, telling me there were a few places in Terre Haute, Indianapolis for me to have a book signing.

Then sometime thereafter we set a date for me to come there on April 13, 2019.

I planned to stay there for the weekend so I could spend some time with my family while I was there.

On that Sunday I attended church with my cousin and became well acquainted with a lot of the members there.

Some of them had attended my book signing the day before.

My cousin had asked me to sing for them, so I did.

Now every time I go there to hold worship services with them, they look forward to hearing me sing.

So, I proceeded thereafter making a calendar up for the places I would go to have my book signing.

These were the places I traveled to: Louisville, Kentucky, Bowling Green, Kentucky, Portland, Tennessee, Owensboro, Kentucky," and back to Terre Haute, Indianapolis.

The Gifts of Praise also invited me to come to Bowling Green, Kentucky to have a book signing at the Corner View Community Church.

I also made an appearance with Felicia Bland on WBKO to announce the book signing.

Shortly when this was over, I continued writing on my second book, trying to get it out in time for Mother's Day.

This was because the book related to the ladies in our society today.

By April 2, 2019, I had published my second book called "Grandma Mattie Goes to Church."

I had finished just in time.

Once again, I started setting up book signings, sharing my creative writing.

"Oh, but you want to know what happens next? Then two of my readers approached me and they were asking me when was I going to write something for the men.

I was astonished to know that a lot of men were reading my work.

So, I come back with saying, "I will have you something by Father's Day."

Then I called Minister Roy Bell, my manager, and I started telling him about what they had said.

He then advised me to write the book on the play you brought me to look over.

He said, "A lot of men are going through this today and I think you will make a great book on it."

I thought about it after having a male perspective view of this book. I would write another book from another play.

While keeping myself close to the computer every chance I could get.

By May 29, 2019, I had published another book.

The name of this book was "Let Me Come Home."

This book was not to bash men or women; it was to help them understand different situations that may occur from time to time.

The question I asked people was how would you have handled this situation?

And then I traveled to Chattanooga, Tennessee.

I must share this information with you about the nice lady I meant in Louisville, Kentucky at Better Days West End record store awhile back.

Her name is Mrs. Annette Morgan. She was there selling her paparazzi jewelry.

We became acquainted, and she invited me to come to her church to put on a play.

I told her, "I would love to bring the cast back to have a play."

She said, "Let me get with the ladies at the church and the pastor and I will let you know."

I agreed, and we continued talking. Then I purchased some jewelry from her, and she purchased a book from me.

We stayed a while longer, then we packed up and left.

Within two weeks I was back in Louisville, Kentucky attending worship service with Mrs. Annette Morgan at God's Will Christian Fellowship church.

This is when she informed me, we could come back and perform the play on October 19, 2019.

I was glad we were coming back to present the play.

When I came home, I called all the casts and informed them of the date and time.

I know that I amaze you at how many times I spend traveling up and down the road, but I have been doing this throughout my journey.

Just so you will understand, this is part of the writing world.

Drive to the different places will give you the will power and determination to rise above what you have set out to do.

This is when you accomplish things like what I'm about to share with you.

By July 9, 2019, they invited me to speak at a National Exchange Club in Hermitage, Tennessee.

I was back on the road again, traveling to Owensboro, Kentucky to have a book signing on July 20, 2019.

Then on July 25, 2019, I traveled back to Chattanooga, Tennessee to appear on the "This-N-That" television show there at the Fox station.

Here is where I had my first break on the Fox news with Mr. Greg Funderberg sharing one of my plays.

Now I was back sharing the book I had written from the play and two more books.

I was so excited about the books I started writing on my fourth book called "Ray Jay's Senior Year.

My…how time flies when you are enjoying what you are doing.

I was thankful again for another opportunity to be on the air sharing my creative writing with the world.

When I left the station, I had to meet with one of my former cast members.

You couldn't believe what happened next that touched my heart.

One lady that I had became acquainted within 2017, who I audition for my play had written a book.

Whitley Love Kaytlin had written a book called, "Living in a Secret Place."

I purchased her book on this day, and she purchased my book.

The story was very interesting, and I was so proud to see her follow through with her dream.

While on my journey I ran into a person on July 23, 2019, for a second offer of making my play into a movie.

I listen to what they had to say then I said, "I'm still praying and waiting on God to move me in that direction."

I feel like greater things are coming soon and I'm asking God for patience, room, and knowledge to receive what is coming.

I know he will not make a mistake if I continue to do what he has placed in my hands to do.

My next book signing was on July 27, 2019, in Gallatin, Tennessee, at the Public Library there.

I was glad to see three of my cast members come out to support me on that day.

Mr. Terry Barr, Minister Deborah Barr, and Ms. Silvia Scott were there as much as they could be to help me in what I was doing.

I can say that I have made some friends along the way.

I have to take this time to share something with you, all of you. In letting you know how important it is not to leave your children out of the mix.

If your daughter sends you a text to ask you, could you add me to your calendar so we can have some mother and daughter time?

This is when you felt bad about traveling so much without her.

"I explained this to her I had no intention of leaving her out of my loop."

So, I planned a day to spend some quality time together while I took my business trip.

On August 3, 2019, my daughter and I traveled to Chattanooga, Tennessee to attend one of Mr. Charles Patterson's plays.

This producer I had become acquainted with back in February 2017.

He had sent me an email a while back asking me to come to see his new production.

I looked at my calendar gave it some thought, then I supported him on this day.

I'm glad we could go, and this play was good, and we had something to talk about on the way home after stopping and getting us something to eat.

It was nice to kick back for a chance to let someone else do the driving for me.

See…most of the time, I do the most of the driving to different functions.

While looking at my daughter across the table I could see that she was having a great time like me.

This is when I said, "We both needed this time together."

On that evening I wanted to leave a word of encouragement to those who all had busy schedules.

So, I uploaded this on my social media site for my followers and fans to read…

Please take the time to spend with your children, love one, family or friends because we never know how much this means to them to know you are there for them and how much you care.

We wind up with having over 65 likes and many comments.

It seemed like they were as happy as we were to be spending some time together.

Anyway, it was time once again on August 17, 2019, to have another book signing, this time in Springfield, Tennessee at the Public Library.

There were two ladies who came in and bonded with me and purchased some of my books.

I was proud to have this chance to get to know them.

We have still to this day been keeping in contact with each other.

On September 19, 2018, I could witness the honoring of my cousin Ms. Wanda Tuck and several other amazing ladies at the Gallery on the Square in Franklin, Kentucky.

While I was there, I saw so many familiar faces I hadn't seen in a while.

One of them was my classmate Kristie Slaughter, who had been in my life since the first grade.

We had homeroom together our teacher name was Ms. Rebecca.

While we were talking to catch up on old times, then she mentioned that her mother was one of the ladies being honored today.

I knew she was proud to be sharing this day with her mama and seeing her accept this honor.

She asked me to take this picture of her and her mama.

I'm glad I did, so I could add them to my journey along the way.

She said, I will purchase your book and I think it's amazing to see you writing and following your dream.

It was good catching up on old times with my friend and adding her to my story.

It was time to travel back to Terre Haute, Indiana during September 2019, for another book signing and the showing of a free movie of "Grandma Mattie Gets Her a Man."

The movie was shown at the Vigo Public Library there in Terre Haute, Indiana.

While I was there, I attended a Tea Party I was invited to a while ago by Ms. Marilyn Strong.

The greatest thing about this day I was on the program to speak.

Yes, I was invited to speak on this day and my subject was "A Mother and Daughters Love."

I had the best time socializing with these ladies and their husbands and hearing the other ladies speak.

I also attended church on Sunday at the Saint John Missionary Baptist Church with Ms. Marilyn Strong.

In between time, I was still writing on my book trying to get done in time for Christmas.

It was time for us to perform in Louisville, Kentucky on October 19, 2019, when I had three people to not show up.

And they packed the place that night we had about 100 people there.

Once again, we four pulled together and put on the best performance that they would ever want to see.

When I talked to Mrs. Annette Morgan after the show and told her what happened.

She said, "Well, the show was good and we couldn't tell anyone was missing."

You all did a wonderful job and we are looking forward to you bringing back Part II.

This was all I needed to hear to make my night complete.

Then we packed up, and headed home talking about our last play would be in two weeks.

We were happy to be traveling in two weeks to Terre Haute, Indiana, to perform there.

This was our last play for the year.

Then it was time to take the play to Terre Haute, Indiana, on October 29, 2019.

So, I picked up where I left off and started back writing on my book.

Then on November 16, 2019, I held a special evening with a few of my family and friends in Bowling Green, Kentucky.

There were refreshments, we played games; I gave away door prizes.

And let me tell you these ladies were serious about these games, they loved them so much.

We even had a special guest named Ms. Marilyn Strong to come, from Terre Haute, Indiana to share with us her sparkling paparazzi jewelry.

They all had a great time, and I had so many compliments on the food.

Everyone left with something in their hand, and I was glad they enjoyed themselves.

Left around to right: Angel Vasquez, Lauren Tuck, Michelle Heater, Leandra Miller, Alice Gamble, Cynthia Ford, Shaniqua Turner, Marilyn Strong, Alexis Smith, Jo Ann Smith, Jerina Smith.

Well, you wouldn't believe it, but when December 7, 2019, came around I had completed my fourth book.

I felt good because I had reached my goal of having it done in time for Christmas.

Now it was time to work on my Fifth book.

I had promised my two cast members, Mr. and Mrs. Terry Barr, I would start working on the book.

So, I gathered some pictures together and sent them to her to get her approval on the ones I would use.

By working together, she shared with me the ones she wanted me to use.

Then I had all the pictures I needed to work with.

8

STARTING THE NEW YEAR OFF ON TELEVISION JANUARY 1, 2020

On December 16, 2019, I decided to send the WNKY 40 an email asking her if I could come on the show to promote my new book of "Ray Jay's Senior Year." They contacted me back with an available date on 01-16-19.

Then I sent out another email on January 20, 2019, asking WBKO if I could come on their show. They answered me back on that morning at 11:03 am with saying, "Are you available the morning of January 1? You'd need to be here by 6:30 a.m. Let me know… Thanks"

I was expecting to get in before Christmas so that I could promote in time for the Christmas Holidays. But instead, I felt like God had a better plan for me; he worked it out so that I could start off January 1, 2020, with another new beginning.

Then I started placing the information on my social media page, through my emails and by word of mouth to family members, friends, and other sites.

As the Christmas holidays past and the time was growing near New Year's Day, I was thinking about what a great way to start the New Year off with being on national television on the first day of the year.

I awoke at 4:00 am after hearing the alarm go off then I pushed it off and reset it for 4:30 am. When the alarm went off again, I got up out of bed and headed for the bathroom took my bath, dried off, applied my lotion, perfume, and then I put my clothes on.

While I was painting my nails I was going over in my head some things I would say while I was in the interview.

My nails dried and then I grabbed my keys and purse and headed for the car to drive to Bowling Green, Kentucky for my interview.

Once I arrived, I parked the car got out and went up to the door rung the buzzer and the lady let me in and I followed her to the waiting area.

After sitting there for about twenty-five two thirty minutes then she came back into the room and took me into where I would give my interview.

They placed a microphone onto my blouse, and shortly afterward I was on the air.

It was finally happening I was on television…live…telling the world once again about another one of the creative books that I had written and published. This book was available on Amazon.com, ready to purchase for anyone who wants to read it.

This book was a book of different situations relating to a lot of single parents who have gone through some things similar to what I had gone through. Or who might be going through something close to this situation?

I was hoping this book could help the parents and the children or child might be in the same situation.

No one can predict the future on what will take place, but what we can do…is share a situation that may happened to us or a friend.

Even though it's fiction, we can write something similar to help others know they are not alone.

Then on January 20, 2020, it happened.

I had once again published another book this was my fifth one.

Yes, I was excited and thrilled to have accomplished five books within a year.

Sitting here looking back over my journey I knew why I had to continue with my creative writing journey.

I was seeing why my purpose for being here was in the will of God.

He wanted me to share my creative writing because he knew I would humble myself and be obedient to his word.

God knew exactly what we will do because he made us and gave us life.

Therefore, it's hard for us to understand sometimes what's going on in our lives, but he does.

Having a connection with God gives us the ability to find out what our purpose is here.

Therefore, continue to pray and ask him for the confirmation that you need to be ready for what he has to give you.

And, he's the line of connection will always be open to you because the line is never busy.

We have to be patient and be willing to wait for the answer he will give us.

I then started thinking it was time for me to write my book on my journey.

They had been asked me several times before when I would write something about myself.

Now after thinking about it, I thought this would be a great time

And this would take place soon, but I felt like I needed to have my special event before I did this.

But before I share this information, I wanted to tell you about the surprised birthday party my daughter gave.

My daughter had asked me if I would like to go to a comedy show sometimes I said, "I wouldn't mind."

We continued to talk about other things for a little while longer, when we continued with our daily life.

Weeks had passed nothing more about going to the comedy show till on January 04, 2020, I received a group text message from my daughter saying, "Hey, ladies. As you all know mama is turning 60 years old."

So, I figured we could all do something together to help her celebrate her birthday.

Angela has bought us tickets to a comedy show on February, 1. I figured we could go out to eat before we go.

So I was thinking we could leave around 4:30 p.m.

"Okay sounds good", said my niece Shaniqua.

Then, my other niece, Angela replied, "Yes, 4:30 will be great. We have to start on time though because I got us the best seats in the house. Also, everyone will need to wear black and gold, it's the theme colors that we will be wearing."

My daughter said, "Ok, cool."

Then finally my baby sister Cynthia sent a thumb up letting us all know that this was alright with her.

Weeks and days were going by as I was making plans for my 1st Annual Valentines Author Event scheduled for February 8, 2020.

On November 17, 2019, I started sending out my pre-invitations for my 1st Valentine's Author Event.

This is something I had wanted to do for over a year was to have something with a group of ladies more on a personal level to share my writing career with.

I'm looking forward to April 8, 2020, for the 1st Valentine's Author Event

This would be my very first big event that I was having for the ladies.

I had planned this event almost three months before it was time because "I want them to have a day that they could feel good about themselves, by being pampered." Compliments from Sarah Tuck Production/Sarah Tuck Books.

Then on the Saturday before my event, it happened my daughter tricked me into thinking I was going to a comedy show and I wind up going to my surprised birthday party blind-folded.

When I pulled off the blindfold, it surprised me to see all the friends and family that had come that night to make my birthday party a successful one.

I could see why the text said, "For everyone to wear black/gold colors".

My daughter had the place decorated in black/gold colors. Everything was beautiful.

It was a birthday party that I will never forget plus seeing all my family and friends was a blessing and the food was good.

God has been good to me and I'm thankful for him letting me see my 60th birthday.

While resting over the weekend, Monday came about, "I started getting things ready for the event."

9

FIRST ANNUAL VALENTINES AUTHOR EVENT

In this chapter, I will share with you how and when I started my first Annual Valentine Author Event.

This event was something I wanted to do for some time now.

I was busy shopping from time to time for gifts for the bags of food table clothes napkins and, amongst other things that we needed to make this event special.

Not only was I busy shopping, but there were a few more people helping me with my event.

Especially my cousin Marilyn Strong, she would call me to let me know what she had gotten, and then a few days later I would call her to let her know what all I had picked up.

She was a lot of help to me in making the sashes for the chairs, the boutonniere for the servers, and she even made some corsages for me and her.

We were so busy we forgot to get them out of the box to put them on the guys.

Meanwhile, on that Friday, February 7, 2020, I was cleaning up the house for my cousin Marilyn and her friend/manager to come to stay.

When I realized when I looked at the time it was getting late in the evening.

I stopped cleaning to go pick up my nephew then we headed to the place to pick up the key to the building where the event would be.

But when I arrived, there was no one at home. This is when I started to panic.

I knew at that very moment that I had waited too late to pick up the key. So, I left a note on the door asking the lady to call me when she got home so I could come back to pick the key up.

We then went to the store to pick up the grocery I needed for preparing the food for my event.

Before I could get back to the house with the grocery, my cousin Marilyn called to let me know that she had arrived, and that she was waiting at my house for me.

I told her I would be on my way as soon as I made one more stop.

When I got there, we all hugged and greeted one another, then we went into the house.

We all sat down and talked for a while when I looked down at the time and seen that it was getting to be almost midnight.

I then got up and took my nephew home. He said, "If you want me to come back out and help you, just let me know."

I told him I would, and then I came back to the house to finish talking with Marilyn and her manager.

While we were sitting there laughing and eating my phone rang. I looked down at it and it was the lady calling me about the key to let me know that she had made it home. She had realized that she hadn't given me the key to get into the building.

I told her it was ok; I would come and pick it up right away.

By this time, I could tell that I would run behind on getting everything together.

I had to go back and pick my nephew up again because I had taken him home earlier.

Then I drove over to the building, opened it up, went inside to only find out the table was already sitting up.

I was glad they were already sitting up. This saved us some time.

Now, all we had to do was apply the table clothes.

I was getting sleepy, so I told my nephew I would take him home, and if I needed him, I would contact him tomorrow.

He said, "Just let me know Aunt Sarah and I will come and help you."

When I had gotten back to the house, Marilyn and her friend had already gone to bed. Then I brushed my teeth and freshen up and went to bed.

"I got up early the next morning to fix the potato salad, Watergate salad green beans, and bake the chicken."

In between time I was trying to fix the Program for that evening for the event. But the phone was ringing, and I was running back and forth to the building to put more decorations on the table and I carried the food that I had fixed out there.

Even on the day of the event, "I was still picking up items for the event. Not to mention I was having Marilyn go out and run some errands for me."

I then went back to the house finished cooking then took more food to the building. I then put about four more tablecloths on the tables, finished adding the place setting to the table.

Suddenly I heard the door opened when I looked around and in came my manager, Minister Roy Bell. I spoke to him and then kept right on getting things ready. When he asked me, "Do you know that it is 5:40?"

I couldn't believe it; I had been busy right up to the time for the event to start.

I stopped what I was doing and hurried home to get ready. I wind up being about 45 minutes late.

I made sure the ladies would have entertainment while they were waiting. I had a band from Nashville, Tennessee there to entertain them.

But it didn't seem to matter much with the ladies they were smiling, laughing, talking, and enjoying the music that I had chosen for the evening.

I made a list of love songs like they play at a wedding from the gospel artists and some from artist that makes loves songs for weddings.

The music was instrumental only because I thought this would be more appropriate for this special occasion.

I wanted the music playing as they walked in, being escorted by one of the gentleman to their table.

The soft music was playing in the background while they were eating, just as if they had come with a gentleman out to dinner.

I know that it wasn't the same but, from what I could see and hear, it was great and loved by these ladies.

Me being a lady myself gave me more of an idea of what these ladies needed to make their evening one that they could always remember.

Plus, I had a guest for the evening, Marilyn Strong with her fabulous paparazzi jewelry to look at and purchase if they liked while waiting.

Ms. Marilyn Strong was there from Terre Haute, Indiana she enjoyed the event.

Ms. Sandra exact words were, "Thank you, Sarah, for your inspiration and your hospitality. You did it up and I know you will achieve your dreams. You've got it."

Marilyn always enjoys herself coming to my book signings and events.

Then I went around greeting some ladies. Then I made my way over to the podium where my manager Minster Roy Bell was to inform him of the other things that I had added to the program.

As I was walking toward him I looked over on the table where Betty had displayed the books. There it was a video of some creative writing journeys that Bettie Ann…my cast members/photographers…had set up on her computer and surprised me with.

I only had a few minutes to glance at it because the ladies were waiting for me to get started. But, from what I could see, it looked good.

I then had Nathaniel Downey and Jeff Spencer come up and get some paper to give to the ladies so we could have some door prize drawings.

Then we played a game where they had to put down their favorite animal. Then write ten numbers between one and twenty-five. Then if your numbers were called out, you had to imitate your animal. These ladies had the best time playing this game.

After the game we stopped to have the food blessed by Minister Roy Bell, then the servers Nathaniel and Jeff had a few of the ladies to go up to fix their plate a few at a time.

Once some of them had been seating and were eating…the gentlemen served their drinks. I then check to see how they liked the food.

They were telling me it was good; I was glad to hear they were enjoying an old fashion home-cooked meal as Grandma Mattie would fix.

I was thinking about how worried I was about the baked chicken wouldn't turn out to be good. But, I heard more compliments out of it than I did anything on how good it was.

I fixed my plate and eat then I paused for a moment to look around and see that the ladies were eating, laughing, and enjoying themselves.

Seeing them mingling with the other ladies that I had invited out of state gave me such joy to know that I had touched all these women lives, and then I made it possible to bring them all together in one room.

This gave me such a good feeling to see this picture of them having fun and enjoying their evening with me, the author...Sarah Tuck.

Some of these ladies rarely got out that much to be in a setting like this. But this was their night to mix and mingle with each other.

There were single ladies, married ladies and widows there to enjoy this special event.

They were loving and embracing one another at my 1st Aunnual Valentines Author Event.

Now it was time for us to have our cake tasting contest. I had the gentleman to be the judges to taste and judge for this prize.

So they came forward and after tasting the cakes to give me, the two ladies were the runner up and the winner for the best tasting cake.

Ms. Mary Whiteside was the runner-up with her Mississippi Mud-Cake they both agreed on hers.

And the other runner up was Ms. Deborah Doss one of my girlfriends from way back. Yes we have been friends ever since six grade and; she has always been there when I needed her. As my daughter would say, "Mama she is your best friend and ride or Die chick."

I love Deborah and I thank her for always being there for me when I needed her.

Both ladies were so proud to get their gifts and were happy that they won.

Oh, but this was just a portion of what happened. Grandma Mattie came in with her cake and had the whole place laughing. She put on a show that was out of this world. She had these ladies cracking up and, even the bandleader, and the serves were in on too.

She had the bandleader to tie her apron upon her. Her exact words were, "Tie me up, Baby."

Mind you…this was all in fun nothing serious.

All you could hear was the laughter and joy they were having while seeing Bettie Britton, my cast member/photographer, perform.

While sitting there looking around this is what I saw. Louisville, Kentucky; Gallatin, Tennessee; Cross Plains, Tennessee; Bowling Green, Kentucky; Terre Haute, Indiana; and Franklin, Kentucky were in the house that night.

This was such a beautiful site to see all these ladies in the same room sharing their love happiness while lifting one another.

Right to the left: Annette Morgan, Sarah Tuck, and Patricia Martin.

Remember, this is the lady I saw in Louisville, Kentucky, at the Better Days West End record store.

And she hosted a play for me.

Now we have become best friends, and through her, I've made another friend with Ms. Pat Martin.

Right to the left: Michelle Heater, Sarah Tuck, Tina Fant, Eldred Knight, Brenda Spiller, and Willie Mae Pheal.

These ladies came through by my best friend Michelle Heater.

My motto is to tell one, bring one, you will bless one.

This event was not only about the author and her books, but this event was for these ladies in red/gold to embrace and give encouragement to one another while having fun.

I asked, and they delivered it to me all the colors looked marvelous on these ladies.

When I was asking them what to wear, they were so excited to be getting ready for this event.

Even my cousin Ms. Mary Mitchell gave us an extraordinary fashionable look that night.

Mary Mitchell is a mother of two, Monique and Rodney Mitchell. She has three grandchildren and two great grand children. She is a member of the Red Hat Society and Women of Focus Book Club, and a member of First Baptist Church in Gallatin, Tennessee.

In fact all the ladies looked fabulous in their colors that night.

Oh, and for those of you that have been following along with me in my creative writing journey knows that I met this wonderful lady in the year of 2018 named Ms. Nancy Combow, who is to the left of this picture.

She has become a friend by showing her love to me, by being there when I need her. Plus, she gave my company a substantial donation to help make our play successful when we came to Franklin, Kentucky in 2018.

Shortly after I met her, she told me I needed to become a motivational speaker. I said nothing only kept quiet to wait to see where God was leading me next."

I truly believe that God sent her to me to tell me that because now I'm doing many things.

As I have stated before, "Be careful when someone tells you something because you never know when you are entertaining an angel that God has sent to you."

She gave me a lot of encouraging words and support since she has been in my life. I love her for that.

You see sometimes others can see in you what you can't always see yourself. Therefore, God sends his angels through certain individuals to deliver his word.

Tami Johnson and her mama Ms. Flora Clanton also came to the event that night it was great to have them join us.

When the show was over and they chose the cakes, then the ladies came to the table to get a piece of the different desserts that were there.

I even had a big pan of banana pudding made for them.

I gave away some more prizes then we formed together to have our group photo made for my book.

Betty Ann even had us take a photo with our hands pointing up, giving thanks and praises to God for a loving evening.

Front row from left to right: Patricia Martin, Annette Morgan, Linda Atkins, Sarah Tuck, Mary Mitchell, Alice Bailey, Jo Ann Smith, Brenda Spiller. Second row from left to right: Mary Mitchell, Monique Mitchell, Dora Calhoun, Alma Johnson, Nancy Combow, Lila

Downey, Tami, Stephanie Downey, Alexis Smith, Sharon Taylor-Carrillo, Michelle Heater Tina Fant, Eldred Knight, Martha Emerson, Willie Mae Pheal, Melinda Turner and Angela Rodriquez.

As I look back at this photo, I can see this is only the beginning of what's coming soon. God has favored me to do his will in what he gave me to do in May 2014.

By making these ladies feel special for a day will still in the back of their minds for years to come.

How do I know, because they are still either calling me or texting me to let me know what a good time they had.

Some have even said, "I hope that I'm invited to come back next year."

I quickly reminded them they were all invited to come back next year and to invite someone to bring.

I just want to thank you God for making that day a glorious day we can all remember.

AFTERWORD

This story was about the author of this book, Sarah Tuck Creative Writing Journey. She has become an entrepreneur while developing skills along her journey. Being a writer takes a lot of thought, patient, and time. Her writing career has given her so much pleasure while bringing joy to people she doesn't even know. And the ones she does, knows who express to her how much they enjoy reading her creative writing and they are always looking for more. While on her journey she has become the producer and director of the Production Company called Sarah Tuck Production, of which she also acts and sings in. Since the beginning of starting her Production Company, she has learned to become an Author since 2019 and has written five books except this one will make her sixth book. She loves writing fiction and true stories about characters and people sharing her gift with them and about them; by honoring them in her books, television interviews and her plays. She is looking forward to the continuation of writing more plays and books as she continues with her journey.

ABOUT THE AUTHOR

Contact Information

Email: tuckproductions@yahoo.com

Facebook.com/protecting 2014

Twitter.com/sarah1057rabbit

Instagram.com/sarah_tuck_production2014

www.ingramcontent.com/pod-product-compliance
Lightning Source LLC
Chambersburg PA
CBHW041353290426
44108CB00006B/132